Requests for permission to reproduce parts of this work should be addressed to the author. Contact information can be found on the author's website:

www.ordinarydudemeditation.com

If you would like to invite the author to speak at an event for your organization or are interested in his personal development services, please contact him via the website.

Disclaimer

Ever see the TV show *Jackass*?

If you haven't, cameras follow around a bunch of dudes as they do dumb things.

This book, in some ways, is a lot like *Jackass*.

In other words, some idiotic behaviors are suggested. If you choose to try these activities, you do so at your own risk.

Like *Jackass*, this book may sometimes try to entertain via stupidity.

So I hope you enjoy the ride.

And along the journey, please be responsible…and most of all, be a good dude, dude.

To my buddies and some of my biggest supporters

Andy, Kris, Chad, Todd, Jimmy, Scott, and Nick

with whom I've shared many fine moments, beers, and laughs on the couch.

TABLE OF CONTENTS

A word from the author

Let's be honest. No one needs a guide to the couch. I'm assuming you understand this book is predominantly meant for some laughs. While it doesn't contain the practical tips and insights my Ordinary Dude Guides are known for, you may discover a few nuggets of wisdom alongside the humor.

I wrote the majority of this book after an extremely tumultuous year. I switched jobs three times, was hospitalized twice, and felt as though I was continually getting my ass kicked by the world. Perhaps I somehow pissed off the gods. The true reason for my 2017 struggles...I may never know.

Writing this book provided me some well-needed laughs and relief as I recovered from the previous year's trials. And throughout the process, the inherent wisdom in this guide became clear—there's something special in even the most ordinary of things and the most seemingly ordinary moments.

The couch is a place almost all of us visit at least once a day. And most of us take the time we spend there for granted. But as you'll soon see, you can do an extraordinary number of amazing things on this very ordinary piece of furniture. I love my couch. In fact, I love most couches. But I often fail to recognize the transformative, special moments that continually occur in such a simple setting. I've had many first kisses, recovered from many heartaches and illnesses, and have shared hundreds of happy moments with friends and family members on the couch.

Through the good times and bad, the couch is always there. Never passing judgement, quick to console in tough times, and always ready for me to crack a beer while lounging on its welcoming lap. While a dog may be "man's best friend", the couch is truly "dude's best friend."

I hope this guide makes you laugh. I hope it cracks a smile on your face more than once. But also, I hope it helps you become more conscious of the amazing things that happen every day.

For the most part, life is nothing more than a series of ordinary days. And it just so happens that us dudes spend many of those days partially on the couch: a place where much of life unfolds. I hope this book reminds you of, and helps you appreciate, all the simple, yet wondrous things that happen here. Enjoy the read.

Rediscover your inner little dude

"The candy shop is always exciting, whether you're five or 50."

-    Jebus McDuffy

Build a can pyramid

It was an art form.

Each can downed with pleasure. Made more pleasurable when stacked side by side, one on top the other, to form one of the great wonders of the world—dude style.

Cans stacked into a pyramid.

The first time you saw one, it lit up your eyes. Sparking an awe no less spectacular than your first nudie magazine.

Each can, slightly dented. Slightly grubby. And with a sparkle that rivals the twinkle in its creator's eyes. Whether each was filled with Fanta, Coke or beer, can pyramids teach one of life's greatest lessons.

The journey is the reward.

PLAYDUDE
THE COUCH EDITION
BEER

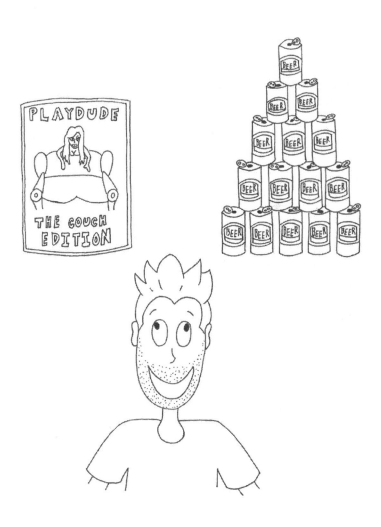

Jump

Wasn't it such fun?

Bouncing up and down, watching *Spongebob*, cracking jokes with your buddies. Living the good life.

Need I remind you the couch is soft. And that softness is versatile. You can nap, hug a pillow, lounge, spoon your monkey butler as you whisper sweet nothings to each other. What?! (See Chapter 60)

But most importantly, the couch's softness when combined with its springs gives you air.

Which means you can get stupid.

Attempting flips, rodeos, or just the classic straight up-and-down jump.

So call your buddies, crack some beers, and go jump on your couch right now.

Count to a million

How many of your friends have counted to a million?

I couldn't imagine a more pleasant place to accomplish such a feat.

Imagine the look on your dad or best friend's face when you proclaim you spent a week counting to a million on the couch. A look of surprise? Shock? Pride?

Possibly at first.

And then their expression will soon turn to befuddlement. What the hell are you doing wasting a week on the couch counting to a million?!

Get a job, dude.

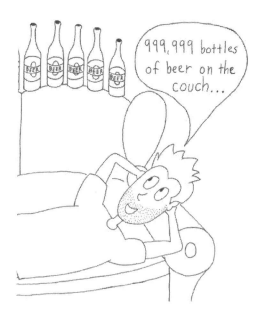

Conquer your fear of creepy crawlies

Afraid of snakes? Spiders? Cockroaches?

The couch is the ultimate arena for conquering your fears.

It's a safe, comforting place for dudes. When a tarantula, python, or beetle is dropped on the couch, you've got home court advantage. Something scary is introduced in a non-scary place.

You got this dude.

Take a deep breath and stare fear in the face. But wait...the thing just crawled under a cushion, disappearing into the inner couch abyss. Shit.

Well, worst comes to worst, if it bites you, the fridge isn't far...

Beer is the healer of all pain, the washer away of defeat, and your best friend when fear wins.

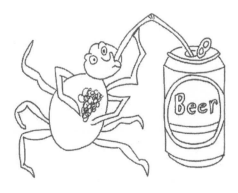

Make a fort

It never gets old.

Even in your 30s, the joy of constructing a couch fortress is still awesome. You awaken your primal, medieval-dude instincts and carefully construct a masterpiece as you stack one cushion on top of the other.

So close to completion, you admire your handiwork. It's breathtaking. You grab your smartphone to snap a selfie and then...

Your nephew knocks the whole thing down. Little shit.

Guess who's no longer going to the zoo tomorrow?

The couch fortress is a time-honored tradition. Nobody flattens it without paying a price.

DUDE

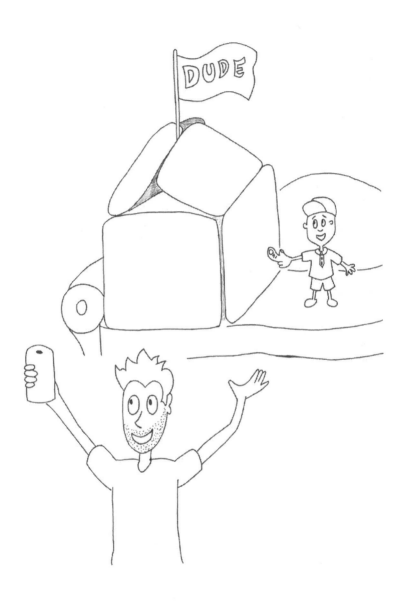

Eat pancakes

Fluffy, soft, and billowy...what food mirrors the glory of a couch better than pancakes?

Oh, the joy of the delightful, circular puffs of goodness. If a couch were a food, it would be a pancake—it is the couch's equal.

On your comfy cushions, it's easy to devote 100% attention to each bite.

You are relaxed.

Free to enjoy the floury aroma, pillowy texture, and lightly sweet flavors.

Turn off the TV for a distraction-free experience. And be completely present as you indulge, one mouthful at a time, in the pancake of your dreams.

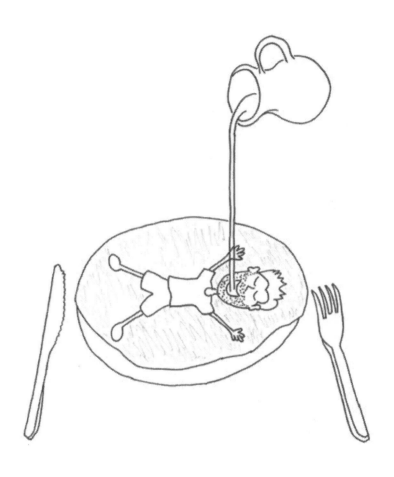

Hold an epic staring contest

Few places are more fit for the staredown of the century.

Think about it.

You have comfortable cushions to relax on. A quiet, controlled environment. And little distraction (as long as you hide the remote and cut the internet).

And let's face it. Some of your most challenging opponents love the couch. Kids under 12 are battle-tested staredown champions...as are middle-aged dudes with ample time on hand.

They'll be glad to meet you on the couch for such a challenge.

Best of all, couch comfort is conducive to a long, dramatic staredown full of eye twitches, false blinks, and maybe even tears. Who knows? Your five-year-old nephew may not take too kindly to your merciless can of staredown whoop-ass.

WHOOP
ASS

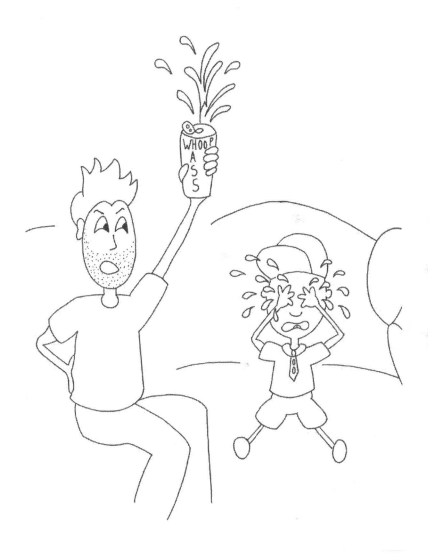

Create fire

Remember the first time you lit a match?

You marveled at the ease of creating fire. Then you blew it out and inhaled a big whiff of that delicious after-match smell.

Once you savored its aromatic burnt scent, you lit another one...and then another...and another...until all your matches were gone.

Creating fire has amazed dudes of all kind, since our caveman days.

Now you can do it easily in your very own home. Just don't burn down the couch.

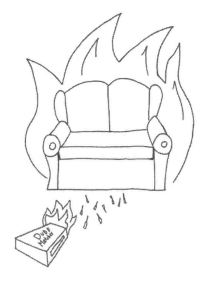

Break a Nintendo

Some dudes like to throw things.

When you're getting clobbered in *Tyson's Punch-Out*, or are stymied by the water level in *Ninja Turtles* for the 50th consecutive time, occasionally you gotta blow some steam.

My buddy Joe throws his Nintendo.

It's a surreal thing.

For those few seconds—from the time when the Nintendo is palmed, chucked towards the wall, and then explodes into dozens of pieces—everything moves in slow motion. As if life comes to a standstill.

And that, my friend, is nothing short of amazing.

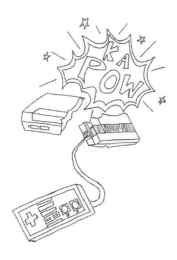

Win a burping contest

There is something primal about a burp.

For millions of years, after a good meal or a good lay, our ancestors have let gases fly out of their bellies, unleashing the roar of their inner ape.

The evolution of the burp is a love story told over hundreds of thousands of years. It began with prehistoric dudes in caves. It was passed down thousands of generations to friars, dukes, and lords in their medieval castles. And today it is inextricable from modern dude's native territory: the couch.

So unleash your ancient instincts and partake in a classic couch tradition. The burping contest.

You think this competition was a fun as a kid? Just wait till you exercise your old dude pipes and mix in some beers.

BURP
BELCH!
500 AD
00
100,000 BC
Today
HICCUP

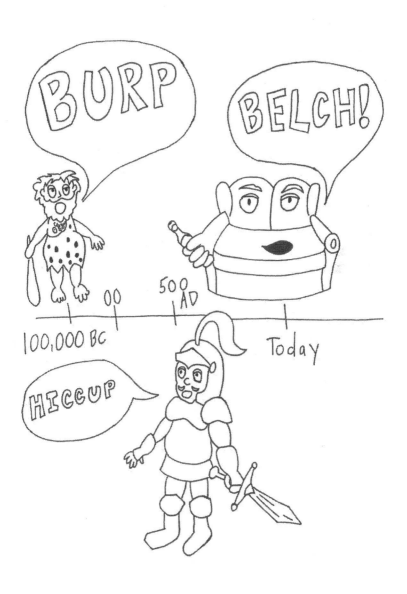

Find buried treasure

As little dudes, the couch was full of hidden treasures.

When your date with the ice cream man relied on one more quarter, when your piggy bank reserves were dwindling...the couch was your gold mine.

Move some cushions, dig your hand in a cozy cranny, or even peer into the dark underbelly between the couch and the floor. Once you get past the puzzle pieces, old corn kernels, legos, lighters, and other mysterious couch casualties, money was to be found.

As older dudes, our ambitions change somewhat.

The quarter, the penny...no longer do they excite us. Yet, there's another treasure often uncovered in the couch's crevices.

When this precious resource is lost, we're lost. When it's broken, our souls are somber. But when it's found, when we dig into the cushions and pull it out, the joy that lights up a dude's face is indescribable.

There are few happier moments than when a dude is reunited with his beloved remote.

Erect a castle

Not only can you construct a badass cushion fort on your couch, but you can also build a castle!

No, not with cushions. But with something far, far superior.

Something colorful, made of plastic, and when hundreds (or even thousands) of them are put together, you can create something grand. Like a replica of the Tower of London.

Legos are amazing things. And no matter your age, they never get old.

Once you've constructed the watchtowers, drawbridge and battlements, it's time to craft the centerpiece.

A throne in the shape of ye mighty couch.

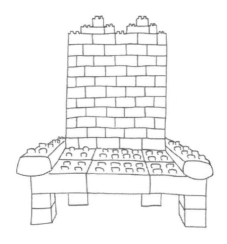

Grow into a big dude

"When the going gets tough, put on your big dude pants and get to work."

-   Johnny Cowboy

Live your own coming of age

First loves, first BJs, first beers…

Often, these delightful experiences occur on the couch.

Let's not focus on only the good, though.

Bad times happens on the couch, too. Breakups, hearing news of a best bud or family member's death, heinous arguments that destroy friendships. All these can go down on dude's best friend.

But is there a better place for all the heartache, joy, laughter, and grief?

Not in my book. For many dudes, your coming-of-age story takes place in the heart of your home...on that fluffy piece of rectangular-shaped furniture that sits pleasantly in front of your TV.

So suck up all the emotion and cherish the feelings— good, bad, but always beautiful.

What do you mean you're not coming to happy hour! I thought we had something here?
BE
Welcome

Watch other people do it

Love it or hate it, porn is an amazing invention.

And how glorious it is that today you can watch people get naked and do filthy things to each other, all from the convenience of your couch.

With rapid advances in picture quality—from STD to HD to Ultra HD, and now Virtual Reality—it's almost as if the pornstars are actually in your room. Sitting right next to you. On your filthy little couch, you dirty dude.

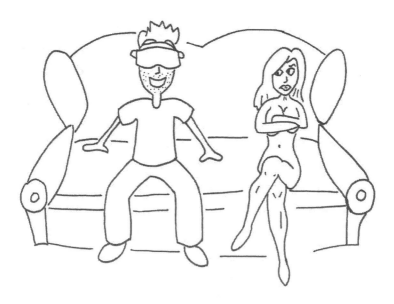

Send sexy pics

With a few taps of a button, sexy pics can titillate your sweetheart.

Oh, how times have changed.

Twenty years ago, it was borderline impossible to send naughty pics. You'd first have to take the photo, drive to Walgreens, get it developed, and then send it in the mail. The whole process could take days. And as George Costanza found out, the pics don't always reach their intended recipient.

But today, you can do the same thing—with a **higher-quality** image of your junk—in seconds.

And it's not all about giving. The law of reciprocity was meant for sexy photo sharing. Give, give, give, and you may just **get** a sexy photo or two. All while smiling on your couch.

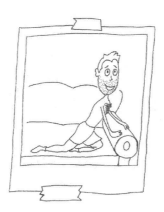

Mourn a tragedy

April 28, 2012.

There I sat, alone in the dark. Shoulders slumped. In front of a blank TV...on no other place but my couch. Derrick Rose tore his ACL. And that was the beginning of the end of the championship dreams I had for my Chicago Bulls...

How many sports tragedies have been witnessed on the couch? Thousands? Millions? Probably more.

Hearts have been broken here again and again. Your team just missed the playoffs, your sports hero suffered a career-ending injury, or your quarterback threw an interception that cost you the superbowl.

Tragedies come in many forms.

But one tried-and-true place you can pick yourself up is right at home. Your comfy couch can calm your frustrations and console you in grief. The couch heals all.

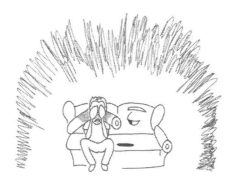

Let mom take care of you

The couch is your recovery bed.

Your mom the nurse.

In sinus infection and in flu, in hangover and in heartache, many a mom has taken care of her little dude (that's you) on the couch.

You watch TV, you nap, you eat home cookin'. Mom takes care of the rest.

Sickness aside, there ain't much better than mom's unconditional love and an entire day spent on the couch.

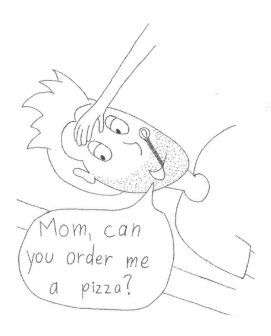

Revisit your lunch

It happens to the best of us.

One beer too many. One tequila shot too big. One view of *2 Girls 1 Cup* too long.

And there it goes.

Lunch is on the floor. And god help you if it's on the couch.

Upchuck is intrinsic to ordinary dudes' lives. Should it be amazing? Well, remember the first time you blew chunks? Had you ever felt more alive?

"Puke and rally" used to be the war cry of champions.

You felt like a hero. And perhaps, just for a moment, you were.

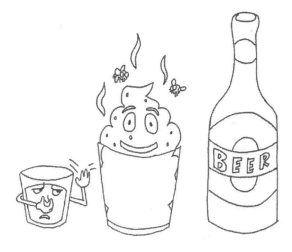

Stick it to the man

Is there a finer place to play hooky?

Perhaps your bed. But as you may recall, the couch doubles as a bed. And that's just the beginning of the activity fun.

You can eat greasy food. Have a proper sit (impossible on a bed). And entertain your unemployed buddies...all fine things you can do on your couch.

So leave the bed behind and welcome the couch's versatility. Wave your middle finger to the man, call in sick, crack a beer, and dial your buddy Jerry. The *Spongebob* marathon is about to begin.

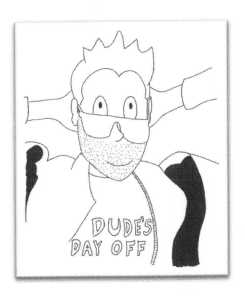

Lose your virginity

Once it's gone...it's gone.

But hey, remember those teenage nights fooling around on the couch?

When a little necking led to something more? Where if you worked up the nerve to go a wee bit farther, you'd almost get lucky?

At any age, magic can happen on the couch. But for many, it's where the magic began...

For dudes who popped their cherries here, you know better than any. Dude's best friend is a damn fine, pretty amazing place.

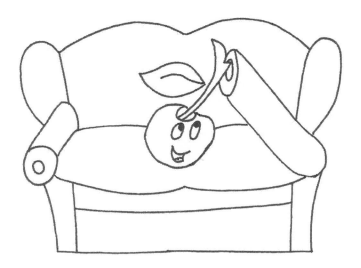

Make a life-changing decision

Big thoughts happen in cozy places.

Places where you can relax, kick your feet up and forget about your job, bills, and the laundry.

Places where you'll have composure to think clearly and can fully unwind.

The couch is your haven. Your sanctuary. The place where big, life-changing thoughts get thought.

So what are you waiting for? Grab a thinking beer and make your first decision.

Sausage or pepperoni?

Yes, it's a small choice, and perhaps not life-changing. But a dude's gotta start somewhere...

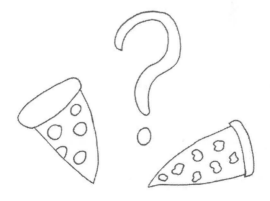

Everyday dude stuff

"Life is nothing but an endless stream of ordinary days."

- Anonymous ordinary dude

Breathe

How easy it is to take for granted the simple happenings of life.

Sometimes the most ordinary of things can bring great pleasure.

Sitting on your ass. Breathing. Being alive.

It's amazing to think of all the bodily chemical functions and processes—evolved over eons—that go into taking one breath.

Best of all you can do it on the greatest place on earth. Your couch.

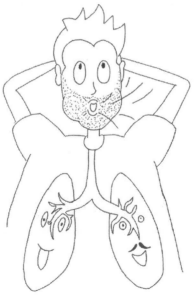

Get laid

Must I say more?

We all know what happens when the bedroom gets boring, the house is empty, and the couch's alluring (dare I say teasing?) presence is too hard to ignore.

It sits there quietly, seductively, in the living room's center. Calling to you.

Its ripe, bulbous pillows exposed in bare sight.

"Who needs a boring bedroom?" the couch whispers to you.

"You're not cheating, you're just having a fling. A little harmless adventure from the bedroom's flaccid confines."

So grab your sweetheart by the hand, flip the bird to the bedroom, and let the afternoon tryst commence—down and dirty on the couch.

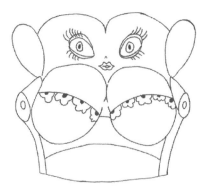

Drink beer

Could there be a more classic couch activity?

All the essentials for a good time are there: ESPN, a phone to order delivery or call your buddies, and comfortable cushions to lounge on.

So kick back, switch on the tube, and crack one (or a couple dozen) open.

This is what the couch was made for.

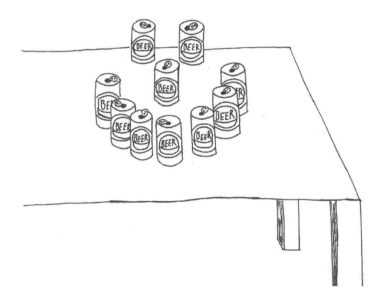

Warm up by a fire

On a cold winter's night, you can snuggle up with a pizza, sling off your socks, and veg on the couch.

Add a fireplace into the equation and new levels of excellence are instantly achieved.

With a fireplace, you no longer need a TV. The crackling embers and flickering orange glow offer ample entertainment. And that's just the beginning...

Call up your buddies, grab some beers and marshmallows, and it can be like camping inside—but without the crappy toilets or windchill.

Cavedudes, Socrates, and Cleopatra likely wished they had a fireplace. But these days, you can have one AND a couch. How's that for a double serving of awesome?

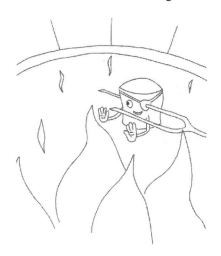

Hand in the pants

When you're ready to take the pleasure of an ordinary sit up a notch, then this simple gesture is all that's needed.

The act is like a dog pissing on a tree to mark its territory. When others see you and your hand in your pants, they know to backoff. You're taking some time for yourself...

To leave your worries behind and slide your hand into that special warm place.

It's comforting.

Just you, your couch, and your hand in your pants.

Some people find relaxation in massage, but Al Bundy and us dudes of the world find it in another place: with a hand in their pants on the couch.

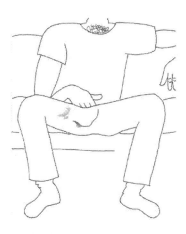

Drown your sorrows in trash TV

Lamar is cheating on Khloe.

Kanye is being a douche. And Kim is just being a straight-up hoe...as usual.

When you see how screwed up reality TV stars' lives are, your worries can easily be forgotten. All of a sudden your problems in life don't seem so big. Or at least, not so stupid.

Trash TV is ideally watched on the couch with a tub of ice cream in lap. It's therapy for the 21st century.

KEN & TERRY'S

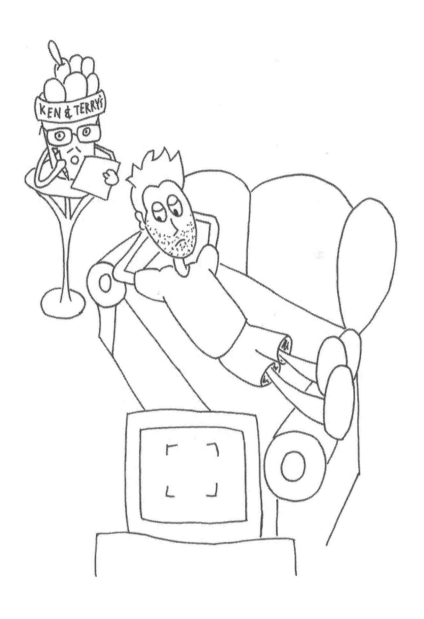

Smell the ham sandwich

The slightly salty, bacon-like aroma of a few slices of pork between two slices of bread.

And the cheese. And perhaps a tomato, melted together with a heavy yet light and refreshing bouquet that wafts into your nostrils.

The circus of smells mystifies, flooding your senses, yet so many dudes miss it. They live their lives running from task to task. Toiling for the man, making appointments, chasing the dollar, and sitting in cubicles. Life passes them by.

The wise know better. They spend more time on the couch. And refuse to let the ham-sandwich smells of the world and other tantalizing aromas escape them. Life is all about the ham sandwiches.

So wake up and smell them.

Just sit on your couch a little longer, open those nostrils wide, and let the good vibes breeze in.

43

Watch the seasons turn

Leaves change color.

White flakes fall from the sky.

Cool weather, rain, and tree buds transform into lush green leaves and hot, humid afternoons.

On your couch, you have a front row seat to the magic of the seasons. And you can witness it all, lounging lazily in room temperature, in between naps.

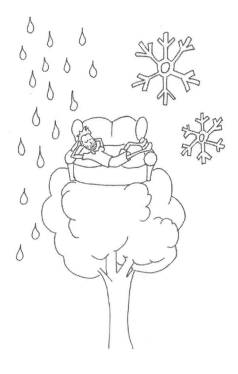

Master the art of crocheting

Grannies have been crocheting on rocking chairs, recliners, and porches for centuries.

New generation crocheters defy boundaries. Crocheting everywhere. In movie theatres, the drive-thru, at concerts, and even on the toilet (okay, grandma probably crocheted on the pot, too).

But old dudes or young dudes alike, the couch is the great equalizer...a comfy, quiet, meditative place where any dude can zone in on a single task.

With your crochet needles in hand, you can crochet your next sports flag, coaster, or wollen koozie. Grandma can crochet mittens.

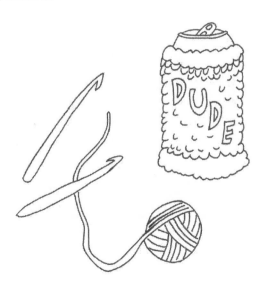

Eat one ice cream cone over the span of 10 minutes

One day while waiting in a Target food court, I witnessed something magical.

An old dude wearing a bowler cap. Ice cream in one hand, cane in the other. Over 10 minutes, I watched this dude slowly eat his ice cream cone, enjoying every lick.

Gentle, graceful, loooong licks.

And then puffing his cheeks back and forth, swishing the creamy, sugary goodness around his mouth.

Then the lick of the lips. And a final pause of satisfaction before his next taste.

His grandson and myself watched on in amazement.

Why isn't all ice cream enjoyed like this? Perhaps it should be. And perhaps the couch is the perfect place to master the art of eating ice cream.

Wear a belt buckle

Did you ever have that friend who rocked the belt buckle?

Resting oh so effortlessly above the crotch, the dude tucks two thumbs behind each side—commanding special attention to his buckle. Glistening in its shiny, oversized glory, the belt buckle could make even the dorkiest dudes look cool for a fleeting moment.

A smokin' hottie struts by. And she double takes. Who is that man with the belt buckle? For once, your looks don't matter.

The belt buckle is the great equalizer. And when you flaunt it on the couch, something very subtle, and dare I say amazing, happens.

Wear the belt buckle, and the foxy ladies will flock like the salmon of Capistrano.

Rise to power

"Achieving great things is best accomplished after a solid nap."

-      Otis Driftwood Beach

Give life

Babies happen. I was conceived after a night of revelry from a Christmas party. Did it happen in a bedroom, on the kitchen floor, or the couch? I can only hope for the latter.

After a long night of drinking, a weekend when the kids are at Grandma's, or when the bedroom seems just too far away, never question the allure of those oh-so-comfy cushions. Generations have surely been created on the couch.

In fact, you may be reading this book only because your parents succumbed to the will of the couch's gentle, soft pleasures.

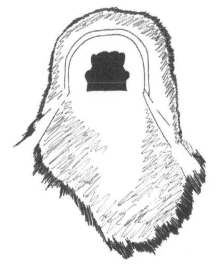

Taketh away life

On the couch, you are the supreme master. You reign over your domain of cushions, empty candy wrappers, and beer bottles. And you wield the most powerful weapon in the coucheth galaxy: the remote.

As such, ants, flies, mosquitoes, and other little beings are visitors in your sanctuary of dudeness. Grant them another day of light, or taketh away life...the choice is yours.

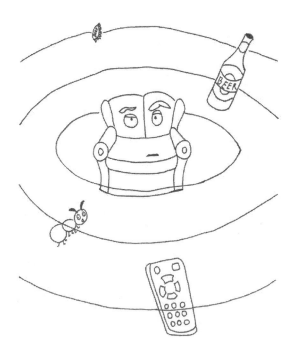

Fake your own death

Tupac may have done it. Michael Jackson may have done it. Why can't you?

Could there be a better place to orchestrate such a feat?

On the couch, the world's most powerful resources are at your disposal: social media, the internet, and fast food delivery—which ensures you're well fed as you carry out the ruse.

Fake your own death well, and you'll not only have a good laugh and great story, but you'll probably get out of work and other commitments for a few days...allowing you to spend even more quality time on dude's best friend.

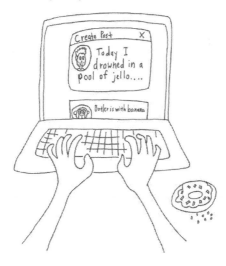

Smash a printer

Ten years ago, I took out a printer with a baseball bat in an alley behind my apartment.

Had I the same opportunity today, it would be in front of the TV on my couch. Like a couple mob bosses, my couch and I would stare the little f'er down, gently stroking our baseball bats in anticipation of the massacre to come...

We gonna *Office Space* your ass.

There will be broken shards of plastic and buttons popped out of socket. There will be ink.

Afterwards, there will be a mess.

But dammit, you'll have a hell of an amazing story.

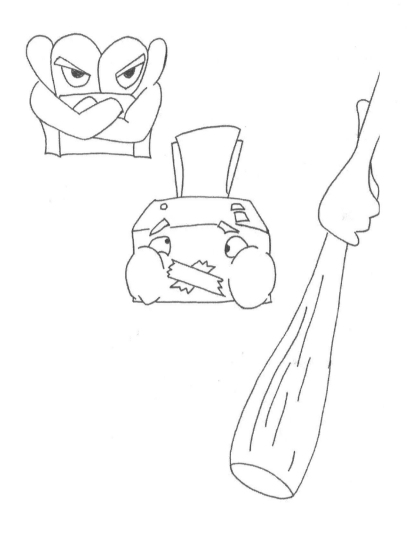

Build a bomb

Not that you would. But you certainly could...

Maybe it's for a science project, maybe you just want to see something explode. The purpose matters not.

The couch is, after all, the perfect science lab for these things—be it bomb construction, brewing your own beer, or solving rubik's cubes. No matter the complex task, if your brain ever becomes strained, the couch is right there to offer comfort.

You can take a quick snooze, order a pizza, down a beer, and then be right back to your bomb.

Be a good dude though, and build and blow up your bomb wisely.

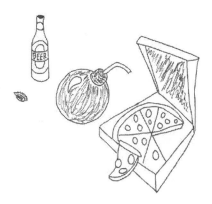

Hide from the law

Sometimes the most obvious places are where no dude looks.

So you did something wrong. You went through the self-checkout and "accidentally" forgot to scan the six-pack.

You urinated in public and got chased by the cops.

Is the law gonna find you on the couch?

Well, it's probably not the first place they'll look...although it may be the second.

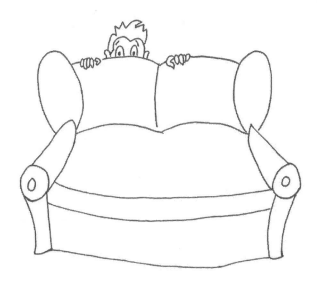

Forge an empire

Amazon wasn't built in a day. Nor was Lingscars.com.

Online empires that drive millions of dollars in sales were constructed over decades.

And while the eBays and Groupons of the world weren't solely constructed on the couch, surely parts of them were…surely.

The couch is a fantastic, comfy workplace to construct an online empire of your own. Much of my budding company was built on the couch. So why can't yours be?

Everything you need for business is right there: phone, laptop, internet connection. Best of all, you don't have to wear pants to this office. On the couch, you can be you— shirtless, pantless, or full-on in the buff.

What can I do to close this deal?
Are you wearing pants?

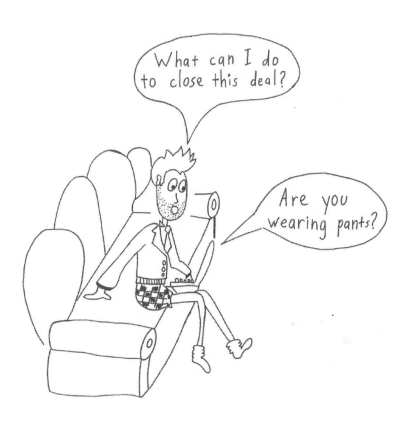

Mock Kim Jong-un

On the couch, there are no borders.

The internet has leveled the playing field. You can mock anyone, anytime, anywhere. Trump, no problem. Clinton, why not? Kim Jong-un…oh, don't tempt me.

Twitter, Facebook, and YouTube have put the power in your hands. You can make fun of, tease or insult anyone, with little to no consequence—all from the comfort of your couch.

And when it's all done?

You can order a pizza. Or take a nap, or just live your life. The couch is the place where you can taunt the most powerful people in the world. Don't miss your chance.

Who you calling rocket man, dude!

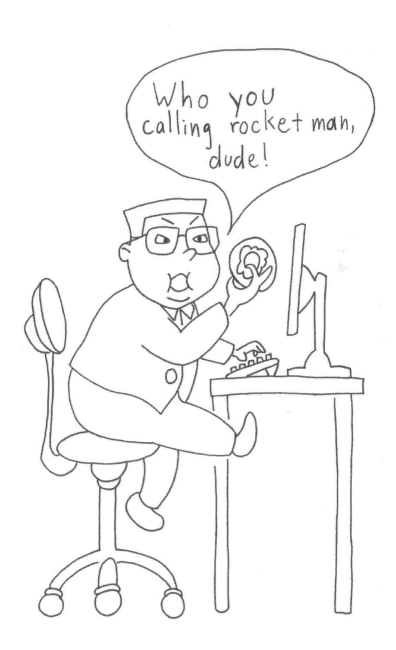

Give birth

I mean it could happen, right?

In the history of dudekind, it's had to have happened at least once! Just once!

In this book, we've gone through all stages of the baby-making process: the exchange of sexy pics, first lay, conception, and so on. It only makes sense that our journey comes full circle. And that's where the really amazing shit happens—a freakin' new life comes into this world. And while it may not be the ideal place to give birth...

You can do it.

Right there on your couch.

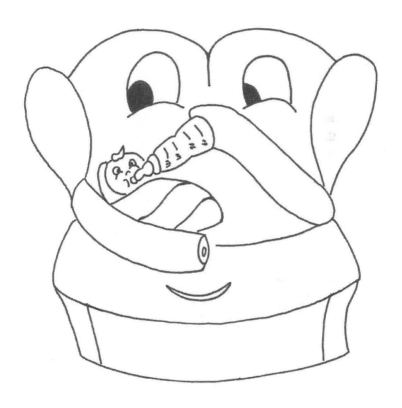

Colonize a new world

Brave new worlds can be colonized on the couch.

Worlds of a different era...like the '80s.

A time when sea monkeys, ant farms, and chia pet ranches reigned supreme under the watchful eyes of eight-year-old plantation owners.

You too can establish your colony. And raise legions of little dude beings who won't understand your commands to grab you a beer or order a pizza.

Instead, you will feed them. You will watch them grow from your couch of comfort. And you will be god unto thousands.

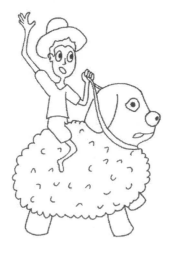

Appreciate first-world wonders

"Give me a Sizzler and a non-squat toilet, and I'll give you a high-five....What do you mean give you 50 bucks? Look at me, do I look like I can afford Sizzler?! I'm from the third world, dude!"

- Anonymous third-world dude

Earn more money in a day than 50% of the earth's population

Much of the world's population survives on less than $5.50 a day.

With a little effort, you can make more money than this pretty easily resting comfortably on your couch.

So remember every time you think life is tough, every time you feel the world is out to get you, every time you complain about your job or messy roommate...look at your couch and smile. And contemplate the money-making possibilities that exist in such a comfortable place.

Remember...first-world problems, dude.

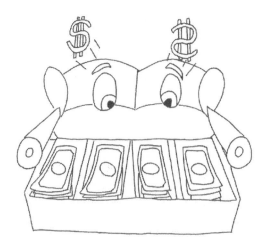

Wear a t-shirt, shorts, and sandals in a blizzard

When it was cold a hundred years ago, it was cold everywhere. You couldn't escape.

If it dumped snow, you'd be bundled up indoors in a fucking parka.

Not anymore. These days, there could be whiteout conditions yet inside you're in the Bahamas—going barefoot, wearing a t-shirt and shorts, watching *Macgyver*.

Central heating is a miracle.

Your couch might as well be a beach chair. Because lying on it, you can be a million miles away from the blizzard outside.

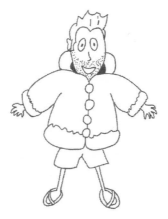

Save the children

Or the whales…

Dudes don't discriminate. There are lots of things worth saving. And by golly, the couch is perhaps the finest place to wield your superhero-like powers. Open your heart, open your wallet, or maybe just type in your credit card number.

The internet is home to countless charities. And in between bouts of video gaming or *Fresh Prince* reruns, a commercial may just tug your heartstrings enough that you pick up your phone and sponsor a child.

And why not? In some countries, a couch is considered the furniture of royalty. So show your benevolence from your throne of comfort.

You can find a cause worth saving on the couch.

Massage

Your couch can double as a bed, a lounge chair, a trampoline, a fort, and more.

As such, this versatile furniture can also be a massage bed. So grab your sweetheart and get them to work on your shoulders, back, legs, or sexy parts.

Instead of paying 60 bucks for a massage at some foreign business, you can get one right at home, on the most comfortable place this side of a sports bar. Happy ending included—free of charge.

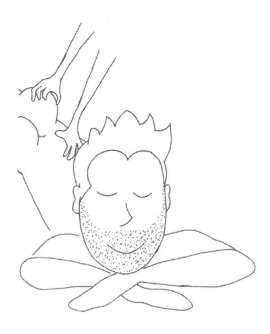

Travel back in time

How does a dude travel back in time? To a day when you were skinnier, more muscular and less wrinkly, and got a lot more ass?

Pop open your yearbook. Take a trip down memory lane and gawk at how damn good-looking you were.

Remember all those annoying problems you used to face? How if Jessie Miller didn't go with you to prom, life was over?

None of that matters anymore. Now you got bills to pay, your own laundry to wash, and the man dragging you down. All those little high school mishaps seem like nothing.

But no doubt it's nice to reminisce. And damn, weren't you good-looking?

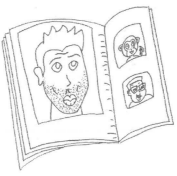

Call someone in a foreign country

I had a penpal once. His name was Ben.

He was in this thing called Boy Scouts Overseas. We wrote each other a couple letters, and then we lost touch...I stopped hearing from Ben. Was it because the passion flamed out? The magic disappeared?

Maybe...but maybe it was because Ben and I grew up in the wrong damn decade.

Had I been born 10 years later, maybe things would've been different. Maybe we could have worked it out. I could have called Ben.

"Ben, what's up dude? Why you stop writing me letters? I thought we had a good thing going."

"Dude, Boy Scouts Overseas has been craaaaaay. We've been working on our Climb the Eiffel Tower merit badge. Do you know how high that is? Like 324 meters! My friend Hansel fell off and landed on a poodle. That dog died."

"Ben, stop. I'm sorry I ever questioned you. I had no idea...what was the poodle's name?"

"Mary Poppins."

"Well, I'm sorry to hear about Mrs. Poppins."

"It's all good, dude. Thank you for your call."

"No, thank you, Ben."

That conversation could have happened had I been born a decade later. And it could have happened on the couch, dammit.

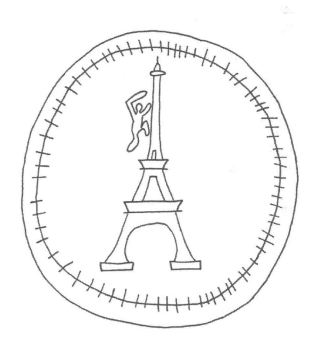

Feast like a king

On the couch, pizza, burgers, burritos, and other mouthwatering greasy delights are never far. Using one of the most powerful devices known to modern dude, you can wield the smartphone to command any finger-licking food you wish.

Word of warning: use your abilities wisely.

With great power comes great responsibility. Too many dials of your magical receptor could lead to an empty wallet, an upset wife, or excessive napping. The latter of which will cause a meeting with the master of an entirely different domain.

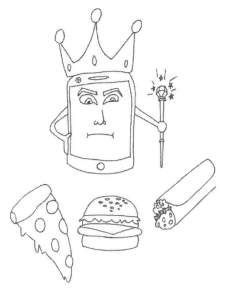

Be eaten alive by dinosaurs...and live to tell the tale

The Sandman is a bastard. You're the king of the couch, but if you nod off for even a second—beware.

Once you enter his territory, you play by his rules.

The Sandman, like any dude, will sometimes wield his power with benevolence. And sometimes he'll be an asshole. Just because he can be.

One day he's teasing you with topless beauties, and the next you're getting mauled by a velociraptor. Dreamland can be a wonderful, cruel place.

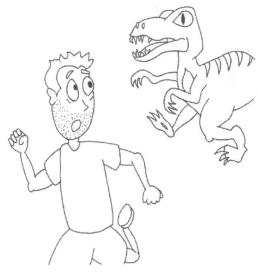

Witness history

On March 26, 1995, Pizza Hut introduced stuffed crust pizza and forever changed the lives of many dudes...along with the size of their pants.

Not only could you witness this historic moment as America's 45th President* introduced the innovation to the world, but you could experience the deliciousness for yourself with a simple delivery order.

When Takeru Kobayashi, the 5ft 8in little Asian dude ate 69 hot dogs—out-dueling his longtime rival Joey Chestnut, and clinching the world record—you could see it on the couch.

When the Bill and Ted's box set was finally released on September 27, 2016, dudes around the world could rejoice in nostalgic bliss. For perhaps just a brief moment, we could bring back the terms "bodacious" and "non-non-heinous", and once again dream of saving a crappy speech with the phrase "San Dimas High School football rules."

Great moments in dudemanity happen on the tube. And from your couch, you can witness them all in their most triumphant glory.

*YouTube *trump stuffed crust pizza*

Become a couch aristocrat

"What if all desks were couches? What if all classrooms had fridges? What if every college campus had nap time? Let's bring back nap time."

- Dr. Bugs Belvidere

Study the greats

The couch is the furniture of geniuses.

Is there a better place to kick off your shoes, recline, nap, and then do some reading?

With a donut in one hand and a Coke in the other, headphones can read you a plethora of wisdom about history's finest minds, such as Albert Einstein, Gandhi, or Chuck Norris.

Whether you want to catch up on classic Shakespeare or the life and work of "Rowdy" Roddy Piper, the couch is the perfect reading ground to awaken your genius.

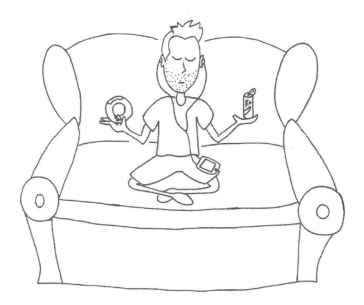

Experience the greatest symphony

Beethoven, Mozart, and Philip Glass can rock your world on the couch.

But it wasn't till the record player went mainstream last century, and joined the couch as a living room staple, that the ordinary dude could experience such a joy. When these two amazing inventions combined, together they formed the comfiest, classiest listening experience imaginable.

In Beethoven's day, dudes would have died for an on-demand couch symphony.

And today, dude's best friend can easily treat you to one...your feet kicked up, butt melting into cushions, as you enjoy a pizza.

Learn a language

Some dudes can speak seven languages.

And you can too, if you want. Of course, you need a quiet, comfortable place that's close to the fridge (in case you get hungry), where you can sit and focus.

And then the world opens up...

Pretty soon, you'll be able to say "beer" in Portuguese: cer vey jah.

Or "remote" in Icelandic: fee yarf steve rink.

Or "who offers delivery?" in Japanese: haisee oh takeyo surushto?

As you develop your worldly, dudely self, you can dream of visiting far-away lands. And if you ever get your ass off your own cushions, you can drink, nap, and couchsurf through any country.

kobliha
chok dee
bier

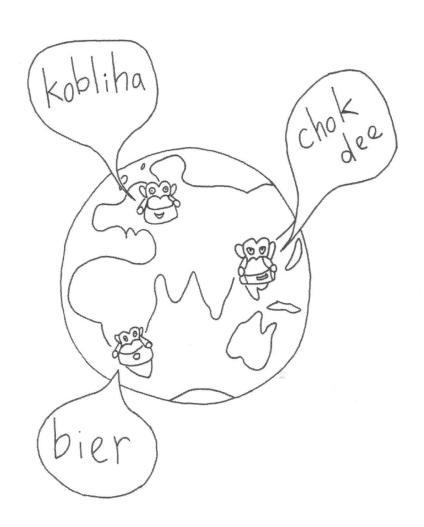

Spark your inner Shakespeare

Today, and today, and today
Dudes sit on a comfy couch all day
To the last bite of pizza crust on Friday night
And all our yesterdays' troubles can fade
On the way to an afternoon nap. Sleep, sleep on this comfy couch!
Life's but a stream of ordinary days
Spent on the couch with family, beers, and buddies. And then the occasional trip to the loo
It's a tale told by a dude
Full of simplicity and six-packs
Signifying the life of an ordinary dude

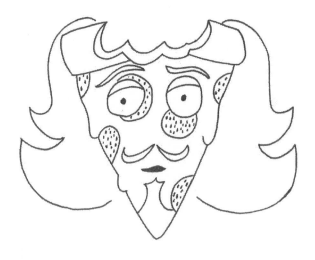

Listen to your inner dude

Your inner dude is home to a wealth of wisdom.

It knows how many beers is one too many, when your off-color jokes are about to ruin a party conversation, and when you need to stop eating the bean dip.

So get comfortable, hug a couch cushion if you must, be still, and listen to your inner dude. After your stomach stops grumbling, gas is alleviated, and you wake from a brief nap, your inner dude speaks. The purpose of your life is...

To enjoy.

Now crack another beer, eat a pizza, and go back to sleep.

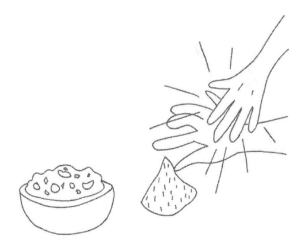

Attain enlightenment

Some say stillness is the gateway to enlightenment.

Or maybe I just said that in *An Ordinary Dude's Guide to Enlightenment*, or implied that in *An Ordinary Dude's Guide to Meditation.*

Shameless self-promotion aside, is there a better place to be still than on your couch?

As you lounge effortlessly on its cushions, the world comes alive. Suddenly you can hear the sound of birds, the rain, or maybe the mailman passing gas as he drops a package at your door.

Your thoughts begin to slow down, your stress melts away, and you finally see yourself for what you truly are: a dude on the couch.

But, dare I say, look deeper...into the pages of *An Ordinary Dude's Guide to Enlightenment*...I digress.

Buddha became enlightened under a bodhi tree. But it might as well have been a couch. Deep contemplation is possible in both places.

All you need is a little quiet. A place to sit. So why not add a bit of comfort into the mix?

Graduate college

Who says the couch is no place for smart dudes?

Those comfy cushions can actually be an institute of higher learning.

Forget the desks, blackboards, and lecturers. In this modern age, you can become a proud college graduate on the couch.

I bet that wasn't possible in your grandma's day.

In fact, I doubt your teenage grandma could've even fathomed such an idea. So put on your thinking cap, switch off YouTube, and get to studying.

Amazingness is going to happen when you become a couch alum.

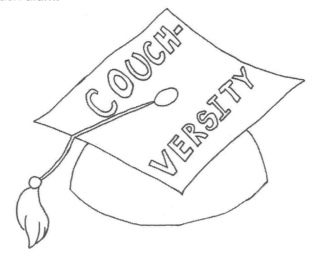

Find your Ben

Mary Poppins didn't want to die. (See Chapter 48)

My friendship with Ben didn't have to fizzle out.

But it did.

Yet...at least we tried for the impossible. The dream of a long-term, long-distance relationship.

Someday I may once again find Ben...sitting under the Eiffel Tower, eating a baguette, drawing caricatures of poodles wearing berets for passing tourists.

The point is this: find your Ben.

Find him on the couch. Don't let him slip away like I did.

Just like the couch, friendships are amazing things. And I think Mary Poppins would agree.

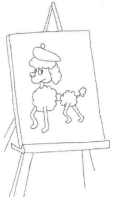

Live the dream

"When you dream big, sometimes you're late for work. Sometimes you don't have time to make coffee. Sometimes you put your underpants on backwards and leave the house. Because a big dream is usually a long dream, and that can cause a bunch of problems."

-    Pampy Weincaster

Have a monkey butler feed you grapes

That's the dream, right?

Forget becoming a millionaire. Who needs to shag 100 hotties? Changing the world seems trivial when a pet primate enters the picture.

Monkey butlers are the ultimate goal.

Think of the possibilities. The endless memes, selfies, and Instagram posts you could capture. And, oh, the activities!

Yes, being fed grapes is a highlight. But why stop there? Dare I say monkey foot massage? Monkey video game partner? Monkey cuddle?

A monkey butler, a couch, and a dude. That's what life is all about, no?

Live the Lebowski life

All the quintessential Lebowski activities can be done on the couch.

You can wear a robe and sunglasses, tell your buddy Donny to "shut the fuck up", and even go bowling, thanks to Wii Sports and other video games.

And when you're done living the Lebowski life, you can cap it off with a viewing of the cult classic, a White Russian, and a nap. Hopefully, when you wake up, nobody will have peed on your rug.

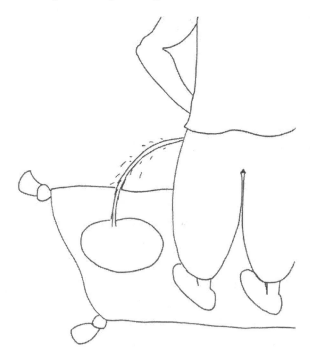

Relive the '90s

Dig out your Michael Jordan jersey, crank the Vanilla Ice, and turn on some *Fresh Prince of Bel-Air*.

Life was good in the '90s. But look...dudes don't discriminate.

Maybe your golden decade was the '80s or '70s.

No problem.

Don some zubaz, bust out your fanny pack, and watch *Alf*. Or blast "Free Bird" and smoke a doobie.

All possible when you relive your glory days on the couch.

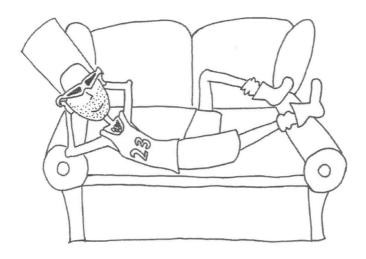

Call Denise Richards

I called her once.

How my buddy found her number, or why he had her number, is a mystery to this day. Why she answered my call after ignoring dozens of my buddy's is another one of life's many secrets.

But she picked up.

"Who is this?" said an oh-so-sultry, sexy voice.

"A college student," I squeaked.

How could I lie to Denise Richards? The truth spoke. And then the awkward silence. A million thoughts rushed through my head. "Dare I point out the elephant in the room?" I must, since this was my one and only chance…

"Is this Denise Richards?"

The phone went silent. And then nothing but dial tone.

I had my answer….

Now...who will you call on the couch?

Well, hello Denise.
COLLEGE

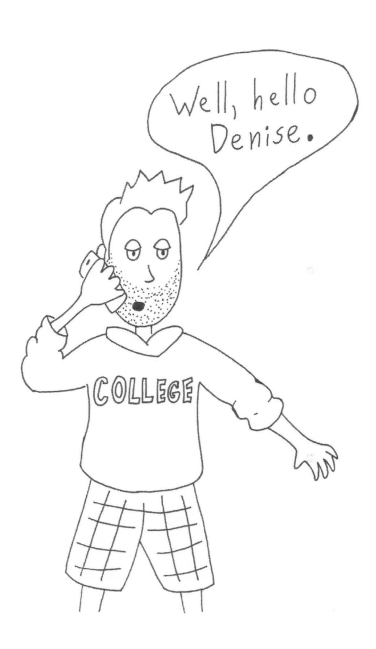

Lights, camera, couch the movie

If you can film an entire movie in one room (Tape, Cube, Exam), you can do the same on the couch. Maybe it goes something like this...

A dude walks into a living room as Pablo sits on the couch.

The dude says, "What, you don't greet your bros at the door anymore?"

"Don't come any closer, dude."

The dude jolts to a halt.

"The couch is armed!"

"Should I call the police?" the dude asks as he starts towards the phone.

"No dude! God no. We can't touch the phone. If I order delivery again, Big Bird said he'd blow me and the couch to pieces."

"Well, can I use my phone?"

Pablo thinks. "I suppose that's alright."

The dude picks up his cell. "Pepperoni?"

"Nah, that was breakfast...shall we say sausage?"

I'll let your imagination take it from here. Just remember, anything is possible on the couch.

So, you thought you could get away with it...
Is that a talking printer?
PIZZA

Be naked

Forget the shower.

Forget lying next to your sweetheart after a lay.

Why not be naked on the couch?

Wearing fewer clothes actually promotes one of a dude's main purposes in life: do as little as humanly possible.

If you sit naked on your couch all day, you'll have one fewer set of clothes to wash, you won't risk staining your clothes with a ketchup or condiment spill, and you can forgo changing into pajamas at bedtime.

Nakedness and the couch were meant to be.

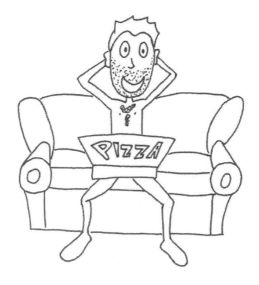

Become a millionaire

An online business can be your claim to couch riches.

But let's get old-school for a minute.

Damn thousands of people became millionaires on the couch before the internet.

The lottery happens. And most of those dudes who win, where are they sitting? Where are they watching the TV in anticipation, or maybe in a drunken daze?

You guessed it, on the couch.

Couch millionaires are a thing. And if you ask me, that's pretty damn amazing.

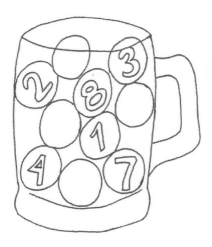

Become a star

These days, anything is possible.

People like Perez Hilton, the Kardashians, and LaVar Ball have become famous for doing nothing. And as us dudes are experts at doing nothing, why can't you do the same?

I'm not suggesting you make a sex tape like some of those above (though that is entirely possible on the couch). But you could become famous for having outlandish opinions. Or snapping cool selfies as you down beers on the couch, and then posting them to Instagram.

And if it doesn't work, what did you lose?

Dudes know life is all about the journey. Time spent drinking beers is never time wasted...unless you're literally wasted.

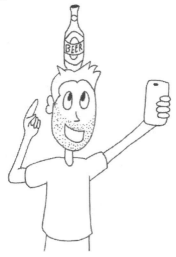

Smoke a victory cigar

Great accomplishments have no doubt been achieved on the couch.

You beat Nintendo's original *Battletoads*, you finished the entire series of *The Simpsons*, or you took a solid nap.

Good job.

Now, it's time to celebrate. Take out those victory cigars and light up.

Relish this moment. Because when your dudemates or sweetheart gets home, they're going to be pissed.

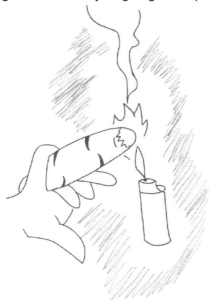

Enjoy a classic strip tease

Surely billions of strip teases have been danced on a couch.

I've certainly had my share.

But how easily do us dudes forget about this time-honored tradition?

Somewhere in the world, there's probably a couch strip tease happening right now. Just think about that for a moment…

Dudes deserve a piece of that action.

Turn on some sexy music, hit the lights, chillax as the stripper struts and grinds to Ginuwine's "Pony", and let the good times roll...

A single piece of clothing at a time.

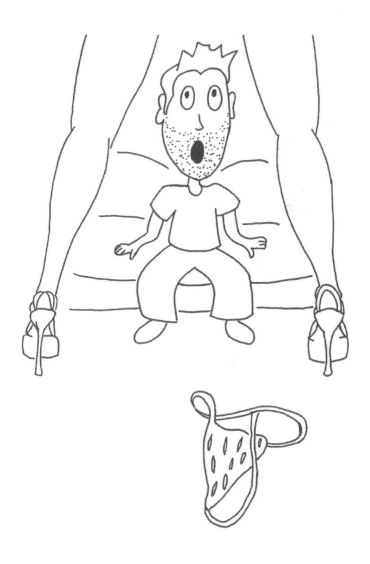

103

Realize your dreams

You've made it through this guide.

Now you know dreams can come true, right in the heart of your home.

From becoming a millionaire to being fed by a monkey butler or chatting with Denise Richards, anything is possible on the couch.

But the story doesn't end here. Think of what the future holds for the couch…

While I've cited amazing technology advancements of the past 100+ years, surely the next 100 will bring even more.

And as dudes aren't getting any less lazy, the couch will be a prime spot for these awesome inventions to happen. You have a front row seat, dude. So appreciate where humanity has been, where it is, and where we will go.

And give some love to dude's best friend. Remember, the most amazing ordinary things that happen every day often occur right on your couch.

I hope you enjoyed this book.

But if you were at all disappointed, I have six words for you…

San Dimas High School football rules!

Also by the author

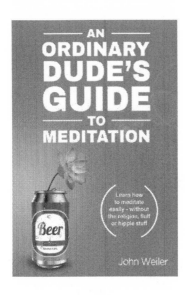

Written by an ordinary dude, for ordinary dudes, *An Ordinary Dude's Guide to Meditation* will unravel the perplexing rhetoric often associated with meditation, and speak to you straight.

Packed with **practical explanations** of meditation's **transformational powe**r and step-by-step **instructions on how to meditate**, *An Ordinary Dude's Guide to Meditation* is your first step to gain all the calm and clarity meditation has to offer.

Available at Amazon.com

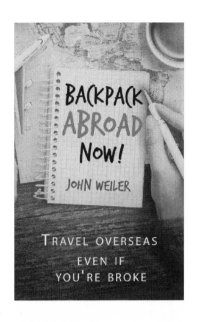

Dream of vagabonding the globe for months on end? Imagine the freedom. The adventure. The new experiences that will forever change your life. But first...how do you get abroad?

Backpack Abroad Now! will teach you how to plan your adventure, **one step at a time**. I saved up for an epic 11-month backpacking journey, while earning less than $17,000 a year, and have been living and traveling abroad for over 6 years and counting. This is the guide I wish I had before starting...when I was overwhelmed and broke, dreaming about traveling the world.

Available at Amazon.com

Special Thanks

Wow. After first imagining this book idea in the Fall of 2017, it's crazy to see it complete. I couldn't have done it without the help of many.

This is my fourth book. And first and foremost, I really want to say thanks to those who've continued to support me throughout all of them. The feedback I've received from Kris Kristensen, Andy Hasdal, Travis Bennett, Scott Pressimone, Pierre-Emmanuel Mol, Dale Jackson, Alex Wong, Nick Zeleznak, Chad Jakubowski, Courtney Jakubowski, and Todd Bogin has been invaluable. I'm sure I annoy some of you guys with my occasional requests for feedback. But I can't tell you how helpful your comments are. Thanks for your thoughtful responses, and most importantly, your friendships. I love you guys.

To my parents, who are supportive of me on this quirky author path. I realize you guys aren't the target audience and probably aren't a fan of all my books, but I appreciate your interest, support, and the fact that you buy copies. Which you don't need to as I'm happy to give you free ones. It's the least I can do for you raising my bratty butt.